Think To Grow Rich - Applying The Laws Of Success And The Power Of Habit In 2020 (Overcoming COVID-19 Crisis)

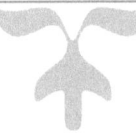

A Self Help Guide To Prosperity And Success In Life And Business

ANDY MUTAMBYA

DEDICATION

"You are as good as a dead man awaiting burial, that's all you are!" When my business partner said these words to me, a few years back, I thought it was the end for me!

Your WHY will keep you going no matter what!

"The life you want, the marriage you want… or the family that you want, is going to be fueled by the business you build." Russell Brunson

"For whom much has been given, much is also required!" I've been blessed, it's my turn to pass on the blessings as well.

To:

My Almighty God, for the wonderful gift of life and grace.

My beloved mother, who is sadly no longer here, for her wisdom.

My beautiful wife and best friend, Elisa, for your boundless support and kindness, and to our adorable son and daughter, Nathanael and Odilie, for your unconditional love and endless laughter.

All of you: brothers, sisters, cousins, my entire family and friends, for being there for me at every stage of my life. There are so many of you that I just can't go through all the names, and I hope that these few words of gratefulness will put smiles on your faces as you recognize yourselves! I hope that you will also be blessed abundantly through these revelations.

And to you, readers of this book, I'd like to thank you and urge you to read on with a positive mental attitude so that you can make the most of the revelations you'll find in this piece of work. **Let your inner greatness shine and inspire others!**

TABLE OF CONTENT

PREFACE

My heart pounded; there was no one I could call. I had already borrowed money from my friends and family to invest in my business, which ultimately failed. I lost their trust when I couldn't pay them back promptly.

Applying the business secrets revealed in this book will bring you success – not just in your business, but in your personal development and ultimately in your life – and help you defeat the COVID-19 crisis.

Are you struggling with traffic, conversions, and sales in your marketing business or as an entrepreneur? Are you having difficulty building a strong downline in your network marketing?

Or maybe you're frustrated that you just can't find the best all-in-one funnel building software to run your entire business! Are you looking for the most rewarding affiliate marketing program or just a passive income opportunity? Perhaps you're a church minister aiming to reach all kinds of people!

Maybe you're struggling, at a personal level, and don't know how to cope with everything going on in the world lately!

This book will help you find answers to your questions and provide a positive outcome, no matter what your goal is

The Coronavirus crisis is a huge challenge for everyone, particularly for affiliate marketers. Many are seeing their commissions significantly reduced and, in some cases, completely wiped out.

Although a few select industries are doing quite well at the moment, this COVID-19 pandemic has had more devastating effects on businesses, politics, and the general public around the world than any other crisis we have seen in our lifetime.

Some experts are predicting that the worst is yet to come… But you don't have to be counted among the victims!

You see, I still remember the day when my daughter asked my wife, **"Mum, you said we're going to get groceries soon, but the fridge is still empty!"**

Without a word, my wife looked at me with that cold look that said, **"Hey, love, you promised that this time everything would be fine. What's happening?"**

"What are we even doing with that eviction notice that we received a couple of days ago due to the fact that we are behind with the rent?"

"What do we do now?"

My dear friend, have you ever found yourself in a situation where your best isn't good enough?

My name is Kalombe Andy Mutambya. I'm an entrepreneur, Amazon bestselling author, real estate investor, marketing coach, and founder and CEO of Andy Mutambya Group.

I love helping fellow ethical entrepreneurs build and scale their businesses to achieve success in life and business.

I wrote this book to help YOU achieve the same success that countless others have seen!

You Suddenly Lose Everything!

What Do You Do From Day 1 To Day 30 To Save Yourself, Your Family & Your Business?

I believe that when we talk about important issues truly affecting people's lives, the least we can do is show respect, honesty, care, and love!

Could this be your "AHAAA" moment as well?

"Not only is it possible, but it is also necessary for you to work on your dreams and to take personal responsibility for your own success in life and business." Les Brown

I wish I knew all the lifesaving teachings revealed in this book ages ago! My journey to improve my life and business wouldn't have been so painful, time-consuming, and costly.

I cannot claim to deliver these priceless teachings in the same way as the marvelous people I learned them from, but I have a valid point to make. Please bear with me and read on with a positive mental attitude to make the most of the lessons contained in this book.

How do you feel when your best isn't good enough?

Have you ever felt as if there is a general conspiracy against you?

"A life without commitment is not worth living!" Socrates

What's your WHY?

It's different for everyone!

You see, I'm a family guy, married to the most beautiful and caring wife in the world. Together we are blessed with two adorable children and I love my family more than anything else in the world.

My plan

When I got married, I planned to provide for my family and protect my wife and our future children, no matter what!

I wanted to spend as much time as possible with my family by having the freedom to work independently from anywhere in the world, without any time restrictions, while providing for them.

My true intention

Out of respect, let me confess to you now that secretly, deep inside me, my true intention was that my beautiful wife and our adorable children always feel secure in every aspect.

I want them to feel that I've got it all figured out and that I have everything under control. Although they love and respect me unconditionally, I always tell myself that I still have to earn and deserve that respect. They should always see me as their hero and know that they can count on me for everything!

How did I go about it?

After losing both my parents at an early age, I struggled for survival while pursuing a better life. I had a good plan. You see, I wasn't born in an English-speaking country, but I managed to secure a place at one of the best universities in the United Kingdom with my broken English.

Nevertheless, it seemed that regardless of my degree with honours, I still couldn't achieve what I intended for my family and myself.

I followed my plan to the letter. After graduating from university, I worked for banking and telecommunications companies, but I was laid off twice - first in my twenties due to corporate restructuring needs, and again in my thirties for long-term sick leave due to a serious knee injury.

As you can see, this plan wasn't working. So I had to rethink my strategy.

Change of plan and adjustments

During the last 10 years, I have initiated and managed no less than 15 businesses, both online and offline, and I did well with some (but not all) of them.

I came to a point where I had enough of exchanging my time for money. I was working away from home more and more, away from my family, and that went against my goals!

My "AHAAA" MOMENT

I had to rethink my strategy again. I was looking for a solid opportunity for passive or residual income.

After wasting so much money, time, and energy searching and learning various systems and products, I came to an epiphany.

I call this moment my "AHAAA MOMENT" because, while doing my research, I stumbled upon a YouTube video through which I was introduced to a training that has since changed my life.

This is one of the reasons I'm sharing this message with you today, hoping that it will bless or edify you as well.

What's changed?

What has changed since, you may ask?

Through the training I was invited to take, I experienced an unprecedented opportunity that allowed me to set a definite goal and focus my mind on my major purpose in life.

Today, I'm a bestselling author on Amazon, the founder and CEO of Andy Mutambya Group, a real estate investor, and a marketing coach with an aim to help fellow ethical entrepreneurs build, scale, and achieve success in their respective businesses and lives.

But most importantly, my major achievement is the positive impact of my work on the lives and businesses of my students all around the world. By ricochet, this experience is also helping me grow even further while allowing me to discover my true self.

I now work independently without any time or location restrictions while being able to provide for my family. Every day I am achieving major milestones I set for myself. I feel truly blessed that through this process I have become a better father and husband.

I'm able to do the things I've always intended to do such as traveling the world, giving back to my community and investing in causes I believe in.

I'm always humbled by the types of reviews I receive for my books, both online and offline.

If this book meets your expectations or blows your mind as well, please consider leaving a comment on Amazon, "Think To Grow Rich – Applying The Laws Of Success And The Power Of Habit In 2020 – (Overcoming COVID-19 Crisis) – by Andy Mutambya" and in our Facebook Group (Highest Paying Affiliate Program) to inspire others.

What's in it for you?

"You have greatness within you to help you be, do, and have whatever you desire." Les Brown

Seeing how this Covid-19 crisis is affecting businesses and people's lives, I cannot afford to just sit back and watch fellow ethical entrepreneurs suffer the way I did. I'm immensely grateful to find myself in a position that shelters me from this pandemic. My intention is that you also take courage and overcome this crisis.

I had endured all the pain of entrepreneurship, then came the point when I had to accept to be helped. It's my turn to return the favor by helping you achieve success in your life and business so that you can conquer the COVID-19 crisis (and any other crisis that comes your way).

I'd like you to have the same opportunity that I had that changed my life and that of many other people!

Apply all of the lessons from this book and watch your dream customers and dream business partners start chasing you. You will begin to see the accumulation of profits in your business, but **most importantly your spouse, children, friends, business partners and all those around you will start appreciating you more and more.**

Please embrace these revelations with a positive mental attitude, taking note as much as possible. It is crucial that you do not skip the practical tests or procrastinate.

When people tell me that my work has helped them achieve their goals in life and business, I always feel truly humbled and blessed. This is my ultimate satisfaction! This is what keeps me going!

Discover and apply the strangest secrets that will lead you to success in your life and business.

But why are they secrets? Because you can ask as many people as you want down your street or in your everyday life, and not many will be able to reveal to you what you're about to learn. It's quite possible that no one around you knows about these lifesaving teachings!

"Make it okay to fail. Don't let the fear of failure outweigh your desire to succeed." Les Brown

This is for business owners in every market you can dream of. Whether you're into:

- Coaching or Consulting

- Local Small Business

- Info Products

- E-Commerce

- Network Marketing

- B2B

- Non-Profit

- Agency or Freelancer

- Blogging or Affiliate

- Or you're just getting started!

This is for you!

The secrets revealed in this book will help you turn on the faucet of traffic and fill your business, website and funnels with your dream customers.

For starters, you've heard about how important traffic is when it comes to building a massive buyers list...

But the question is - HOW?

Well, your struggle ends here because you'll find the ultimate solution in this book.

In this book you get the master key to 'weathering the storm' and getting everything you want.... this is the exact BLUEPRINT effective entrepreneurs, marketers, salesmen and saleswomen use to solve traffic and conversion problems!

You need to realize that what you are about to learn is a powerful kickstart to get you moving forward quickly. You will be equipped with a day by day roadmap to follow to get you from where you are today, to where you want to be!

Ladies and gentlemen, "Hakuna Matata!"

Sit Tight, Learn, and Enjoy!

How Can You Be Successful In Life And Business?

Implement The Key Habits Of Highly Effective People!

Why are some people successful at all they do? Why do others tend to always fail? Your only limitations are the ones you set up in your own mind. Through this book, my mission is to help you attain your blessings.

What is success?

Earl Nightingale:

"If a man is working towards a pre-determined goal and knows where he's going, that man is a success and if he's not doing that, he's a failure."

"A man who is progressively realizing a worthy ideal is a success!"

A man who succeeds is the one who says, "I'm going to become this," and then gets busy working toward that goal.

A person intentionally doing a pre-determined job, whether he is a teacher, cashier, or a nurse, is a success.

Only 1 person out of 20 does that. So why are some people successful at all they do? And why do others tend to fail all the time?

It is because of goals!

People with goals succeed because they know where they're going.

Why do men with goals succeed in life and why do those without goals fail?

Make doubts and fears things of the past. Here is the key to success and failure:

"We become what we think about the most."

"A man is what he thinks about all day long."

"Human beings can alter their lives by altering the attitude of their minds."

"If you only care about the result, you'll certainly attain it; if you wish to be rich, you will be rich; if you wish to be learned, you will be learned; if you wish to be good, you will be good. Only you must then wish for these things and wish for them consistently."

MARC 9:23: "... All things are possible to him that believes."

Napoleon Hill:

"The master key to the attainment of your desires, whatever they may be: Whatever the mind can conceive and believe, the mind can achieve. Whatever your mind feeds upon, your mind attracts to you - definiteness of purpose."

Law of prosperity and success

"If you think in negative terms, you'll get negative results, and if you think in positive terms, you will achieve positive results."

Three words "BELIEVE AND SUCCEED."

Note that the opposite of courage is not cowardice; it is conformity! Outer-directed people are people who think their life is led by circumstances, by outside events they have no control over.

If you can't find the circumstances you want, you must make them. We become what we think about. If you're thinking about a concrete and worthy goal, you'll most certainly achieve it with the right attitude and actions.

A man without a goal is a man whose thoughts are based on anxiety, confusion, and worry. He will become what he thinks about and end up with more frustration. If he thinks about nothing, guess what! He becomes nothing.

Compare a human mind with the land in which a farmer decides to plant his or her crops. The mind, just like the land, doesn't care what you plant in it. It simply returns what you plant.

"As you sow, so shall you reap," as the Bible says.

Remember the land doesn't care; it will return abundance or poison, depending on what you plant in it. The human mind is far more fertile than the land! It's up to you to plant success or failure or confusion or misunderstanding or fear or anxiety… but whatever we plant, it will return to us.

The human mind is an unexplored continent.

It contains riches far beyond imagination…

Why don't people use their mind more?

Our mind comes with standard equipment at birth; it's free. Anything worthy for us came to us free, but we're wrongly programmed to think that the things we spend money on are more valuable, which isn't true!

Our body, breath, soul, dreams, intelligence, love of family, children, and friends... all these priceless possessions are given to us for free! But things that cost us money are actually very cheap and can be replaced at any time. A good man can be completely wiped out and make a fortune again and again. But we can never replace the things we got for free.

The human mind isn't used as it should be because we take it for granted! We use it for little jobs instead of using it for bigger and more important ones. It's been proven that most humans only operate at 10% of their ability.

Envision your goal in your mind. It's the most important decision you'll make in your entire life. Work steadily towards that goal! It will come true. There's no way it cannot – it's a law, just like the law of gravity. See yourself as if you've already achieved this goal and it will become a reality.

Every one of us is the sum total of his own thoughts.

We live off the fruits of our thoughts.

You're guided by your mind

You're in the driver's seat of this wonderful power of your mind. Control it! The strangest secret in the world, the very law that gives us success, is a two-edged sword! We must control our thinking. The same law that can lead a man to success and happiness can also lead him to the opposite. It's about how he chooses to use it, for good or for bad.

Life should be an exciting adventure; it should never be dull.

A man should be excited to get out of bed every morning.

"As you believe so shall it be done onto you," declares my holy book.

Warning! Newton states that "For every action, there is an equal and opposite reaction." We can achieve nothing without paying the price.

To be successful at selling our way to a good life, we must be willing to pay the price!

What is the price to live a good life?

- First, it's about understanding emotionally as well as intellectually that we literally become what we think about. We must control our thoughts to control our lives while understanding fully that as you sow, so shall you reap

- You need to realize that your limitations are self-imposed

- Rise above prejudice

- Refuse to believe that there may be some circumstances strong enough to defeat you in the accomplishment of your purpose

- Act promptly and accurately whenever needed

- SAVE AT LEAST 10% OF WHAT YOU EARN

- No matter your present job, it has enormous possibilities if you're willing to pay the price

Try this practical test:

Apply a 30-day test to the following

- You will become what you think about

- Imagination: control your imagination by controlling

  your mind

- Courage: concentrate on your goal every day

- Save at least 10% of your earnings, and

- Action: Remember, ideas are worthless unless we act on them.

Knowledge on its own is not power!

Knowledge + Action = True Power

Your success will depend on the amount of work you put in. Note that each of us wants something.

On a card, write what you want more than anything else. This could be: to double your income, make a specific amount of money, maybe buying a beautiful home, success at your job or a particular position in life or, a more harmonious family...

Each of us wants something! Write down specifically what it is that you really want. Look at your card as many times a day as you can. Remember, you must become what you think about the most; as you think about that goal, you start to realize that soon it'll be yours.

Look at the abundance around you as you go about your daily business.

You have the right to this abundance just like any other living creature.

Form your habit

This is probably the hardest step, but once you form your habit, it will follow you for the rest of your life.

- <u>Stop thinking about what you fear</u>

There will be a time when you feel like giving up. It's easier for human beings to think negatively than positively. Each time a fear or frustration comes in, replace it with your worthwhile goal.

You must now begin to place yourself in the group of the 5% of the population who are successful. For 30 days, you must take control of your mind. Only think about what you really want. Each day for this 30-day test, do more than you have to do. Give more of yourself than you've ever done before.

Your return in life will be in direct proportion to what you give.

Remember, the moment you decide on a goal, you're immediately a successful person. You put yourself in that rare category of successful people who know where they're going.

For every 100 people, you belong to the top 5!

Don't concern yourself too much about how you're going to achieve your goal. Leave that completely to a power greater than yourself. All you have to do is know where you're going and the answers will come to you of their own free will.

Remember these words: *"Ask and you shall be given, seek and you shall find, knock and the door shall be open to you."* It's as marvellous and as simple as that; in fact, it's so simple that all you need to understand is: HAVE A PURPOSE AND FAITH.

Don't go out in a hectic fashion, but with calmness and cheerfulness, telling yourself that time well spent will give you the abundance that you want. No matter your job, do it as you've never done it before for 30 days. Act as though it is impossible to fail!

By being persistent, you're demonstrating faith!

If over the 30 days, you find yourself overwhelmed by negative thoughts, start over and go on for 30 more days. Gradually, your new habit will form until you find yourself among the select few for whom nothing is impossible.

On one side of the card, write your goal. On the other side, write, *"Ask and you shall be given, seek and you shall find, knock and the door shall be open to you."* In your spare time, read inspirational books like the Bible. Remember: Nothing great was ever accomplished without inspiration.

Above all, don't worry! Worry brings fear and fear is crippling. Remember to keep calm and cheerful. Don't let petty things annoy you. If you sow positive thoughts, your life will be cheerful, successful, and positive! No one wants to be a failure, but remember, you must reap what you sow!

The question is, though: What are you sowing?

You want to make or earn money?

The only way to earn money is by providing services and products needed and useful to others. You exchange your products or services for the other person's money.

- Financial situation

Therefore, the law is that:

"Your financial situation will be in direct proportion to your provided services or products."

- Success and money

People wrongly believe that you're successful if you earn a lot of money! Note: "Success is not the result of making money, making money is the result of success." And, "Success is in direct proportion to the services or products that you provide, and which are able to solve people's problems."

The truth is that you can only earn money after you're successful! It's like a man standing in front of a stove and saying, "Give me heat and then I will light the wood." It doesn't work that way. We've got to put the fuel in first before we can expect any heat. Likewise, we've got to be of service first before we can expect to be paid.

Your success will be measured by the quality and quantity of the service you render; money is just a unit of measure for that service.

- <u>Prosperity and abundance</u>

Don't concern yourself with the money; be of service first. Work, dream, create, and you'll find that there is no limit to the prosperity and abundance that will come to you.

Prosperity is founded upon the law of mutual exchange;

any person who contributes to prosperity must prosper himself or herself.

Sometimes the return will not come directly from those you serve, but it must come to you from someplace; that is the law! Remember, for every action, there is an equal and opposite reaction. A man can only become rich if he enriches others. There are no exceptions to this rule!

If you want more, you must increase the provided service! This is the price you must pay for what you want. If you believe you can enrich yourself by deluding others, you will only end up deluding yourself!

As long as you breathe, you will get back what you put out. Prisons and streets are filled with people trying to make new laws just for themselves; we may avoid the laws of men, but there are greater laws that cannot be broken.

Steps for success

- Set a definite goal

- Quit running yourself down and FOCUS!

- Stop thinking of all the reasons why you cannot and replace them with all the reasons why you can

- Trace your attitude back to your childhood and imagine the time you got the idea that you couldn't be a success

- Change the image you have of yourself by writing down and incorporating a description of the person you'd like to become

- Act the part of the successful person you have decided to become

- Pay the price by becoming the person you want to become

Do your 30-day test, then repeat it if need be, then repeat it again, UNTIL it eventually becomes a part of you. You'll wonder how you could've lived any other way. Take courage and remember that it's not nearly as difficult as living unsuccessfully. Live this new way until the floodgates of abundance will pour over you more riches than you ever dreamed of.

How about money? Yes, expect to receive plenty of it. But most importantly, you will have peace. You'll be one of the few people who lead a calm, cheerful, and successful life.

Start today! You have nothing to lose! But you have a life to win.

Remember, Earl Nightingale states,

"Success is the progressive realization of a worthy ideal."

Proverbs 29:18 declares,

"Where there is no vision the people perish, but he that keeps the laws of God happy is he." The Holy Book also proclaims, "Be renewed by the renewal of your mind."

Hence, this profound statement by Napoleon Hill:

"Whatever the mind can conceive and believe, the mind can achieve!"

This is true regardless of how many times you may have failed before!

A Step-By-Step Guide To Help You Think In Such A Way That You Can Grow Rich

The Seven Principles of Success

The first principle: The master key to the attainment of your desires

The master key to the attainment of your desires, whatever they may be: *Whatever the mind can conceive and believe, the mind can achieve.* Whatever your mind feeds upon, your mind attracts to you: You must have definiteness of purpose.

We receive two sealed envelopes at birth

1. In the first envelope are the riches or blessings you will enjoy if you take possession of your mind and direct it to your own choice:

- Sound health

- Peace of mind

- Love

- Freedom from fear and worry

- Positive mental attitude

- Material riches of your own choice and quantity

2. The second envelope is labelled, "The penalty or price that you will pay for failing or neglecting to control your mind":

- Ill health

- Worry

- Indecision and doubts

- Frustration and discouragement

- Poverty and wants

- Evils consisting of jealousy, anger, envy, and superstition

Write down what you desire and what you intend to give to obtain what you desire.

The second principle: The mastermind principle

This is the principle in which you may borrow the education, skills, experience, or money from other people to achieve your purpose. Being and working in harmony with others.

Let me show you how you can:

- Write your own price tag

- Fix your own wages

- Establish your working hours

- Give yourself financial independence

During the next 3 years:

1. Decide where you wish to be and what you wish to be doing

2. Decide how much money you desire to be making and what you will do to earn it

3. Mastermind alliance with at least one person within your family and another person to whom you're selling your services

There is nothing you obtain from nothing. There is a price to pay, so remember the above 3 steps. Be kind to everyone, friendly and agreeable, and you'll get the same in return.

Your mental attitude is the only thing over which you have complete control, yet it is your mental attitude that has led you to where you are and who you are now. You can direct your future by deciding to control your mental attitude.

Remember that:

- Success must be claimed

- Success must be earned in advance

- Success can only be achieved by taking others along with you

- Success is about getting what you want out of life without violating the rights of others, but by helping them

- Luck, on the other hand, is something you can create for yourself by following these rules

What did Henry Ford have more than all the others to make him so industrially successful?

Remember, your only limitation is the one you self-impose!

Third principle: The habit of going the extra mile

Provide more and better service than others, rendering it in a positive mental attitude.

QQMA Formula

QQMA means: The **Quality** of service you render, plus the **Quantity** of the rendered service, plus the **Mental Attitude** with which you render your service will determine the pay you get for your service.

The QQMA formula is about writing your own price tag. It is an attitude of self-advancement.

Successful people follow the QQMA formula, whether they are aware of it or not. Going the extra mile will make you indispensable, improve your personality, develop a keen and alert imagination, leadership, develop greater self-reliance, and master the distractive habit of procrastination.

It makes others respect your integrity and increases their willingness to cooperate with you. It helps you develop definiteness of purpose and encourages you to take personal initiatives instead of waiting for someone to tell you what to do.

It helps you excel in your chosen field and allows you to write your own ticket while providing a good reason to ask for a promotion or better pay. It conditions you to maintain a mastermind alliance with others.

A farmer must prepare the land before planting his seeds at the right season without compensation of any kind. He then leaves the job to nature and waits.

The principle of going the extra mile applies to services rendered, as in the case of the farmer, whether you are in business or your job.

Anytime we can copy Mother Nature's habits, we can never go wrong!

Practically:

Do this 7-day test: For 7 days, render service to someone who didn't expect it from you and don't expect compensation. Instead, do it with a cheerful and positive attitude. Do not tell anyone what you're working on and by the 7th day, you will enjoy better relationships with those around you and to whom you're rendering the service.

You will then be within reach of the supreme success. If you believe it, you can do it!

Fourth principle: Applied faith

This is the mental attitude in which you clear your mind of all fears, doubts, frustrations, worry, anxiety, and focus on the attainment of whatever you desire in life.

Applied faith is a mental attitude we must cultivate and maintain before we can take possession of our minds.

There are two ways you can use faith:

- You can put it in reverse gear and use it negatively by allowing your mind to dwell on things you do not want such as defeat, failure, fear, and so on like the majority of people. This is the reason why many people are not living the life they want.

Or

- You can take possession of your mind and direct it to those riches, as mentioned before, which came with you at birth in a sealed envelope (sound health, positive mental attitude, love, material riches of your choice, freedom from fear and worry, etc....)

One thing that differentiates the successful person and a failing one:

Successful people all have in common the capacity for belief. The failures will see the hole in a doughnut but fail to see the actual doughnut around the hole. Successful people see the hole but also see the doughnut around the hole.

Henry Ford **believed** he could make a self-propelled vehicle to replace the horse and buggy at the ridicule of his friends and family and without the capital or a formal education.

Belief is the magic word for success. It is the basis of civilization. It is a quality you must develop before you can make use of the master key to success.

To be successful, you must become a person with a great capacity of belief, and you must start with yourself.

Begin by recognizing that you were born with the capacity of complete control over your own mind. You must also believe that by making use of these principles, you can obtain your desires in life.

Always demand, never beg. The Creator never intended for you to beg for anything. He wouldn't have blessed you with full control over your own mind.

If your life is not what you wanted it to be, you can change it by embracing faith and directing your mind to things that you want and eliminating the things you do not want from your thoughts.

You can avoid poverty, fear, illiteracy, superstition, and all such negativities. Deliver yourself and embrace all the blessings our Creator intended for every person on this earth.

Applied faith is the only means by which the master key to success can be applied. Therefore, do the following:

- Know what you want and believe you can and will get it

- Expressions of gratitude for receiving that which you desire even before you actually get physical possession of it. Possession starts first in the mind!

- Keep your mind open from within. When you're inspired to take action, do not wait, but move at once. Remember: **there cannot be applied faith without action!**

- Accepting and surviving defeat: See defeat as a challenge to keep trying with faith

- A burning desire for what you want is the starting point for applied faith; be definite, believe, and act

- When doubt creeps in, remember that:

- As you believe, so shall you reap

- Faith is not something you get; you already have it, but you may be using it in reverse gear by focusing on things you do not want

- Faith is guidance only; it's not the power that will bring you what you want, but it is the power to guide you to go after what you want

- Your faith is limited only by your capacity to believe, therefore believe and you shall receive

- Your life is what you make it by your own mental attitude

Fifth principle: Are people attracted to you?

What is your trademark? What distinguishes you from others?

You should see your personality like others see it, so that you may improve it.

Personality consists of:

- Traits and

- Characteristics

Traits

Every trait in your personality is under your control.

1. The most important trait of your personality is your mental attitude

This is a trait in your personality that will attract people to like or dislike you. Your mental attitude must be positive if you want people to be attracted to you.

How do people know about your mental attitude?

Is it by telepathy?

You disclose your mental attitude:

- By the tone of your voice, whether it is pleasant or harsh

- By the expression of your face, whether it is soft and pleasing, and

- By the courtesy and consideration you give to people

There is no escape from revealing your mental attitude to the people around you

2. The other trait of your personality is the flexibility of your mental attitude

This means that you're able to adjust yourself in all circumstances related to your relations with others without losing your composure or allowing yourself to be irritable or angry. If you have the flexibility of mental attitude, it's impossible for anyone to make you angry without your consent.

You cannot control the actions of other people, which may make you angry, but you can control your reactions.

3. The third trait of your personality is your ability to control your enthusiasm

Uncontrolled enthusiasm makes people boresome. You must be able to turn enthusiasm on and off just like you do with your tap of water.

4. The fourth trait of a pleasing personality is sincerity of purpose

Insincere people will soon be detected and rejected. No one accepts deceptive people around them.

Insincerity carries with it some warning signs that other people can discover.

Most destructive habits to avoid

If you find yourself in one of these, you can rebuild your personality by fixing the following:

- Breaking in and running away with conversations when others are speaking

- Sarcasm

- Vanity expressed by either words or actions

- Indifference in listening when others are. It is more pleasing to be a good listener than a good talker

- The attempt of flattery will bring quick resentment from others. It signals that the flattcrer wants to have something that they do not deserve

- The habit of finding fault in others all the time. It's far better to converse about things that are right than things that are wrong

- Challenging those with whom you do not agree just for argument's sake

- Volunteering unsolicited advice to others

- The habit of speaking of one's physical illness. Do your best to talk about things that spark interest for those you are engaging in conversations with

- The habit of conveying an impression of superiority through the use of words and topics others may be unaware of is a sure way to destroy your popularity. You must negotiate with others at a level that they understand. Truly pleasant people are known to be generous, sympathetic, and in connection with the good fortune of others

Clothes don't make a man, but they can help to start a good connection if they are appropriately worn. Also, make sure that your posture is appropriate and respectful. Remember, if you're not liked by other people, there must be a reason that you can detect and correct. To be of a pleasing personality will require courage and honesty with yourself.

The sixth principle: Self-discipline

Self-discipline is about developing and mastering positive habits. To exercise self-discipline, this is what you need to do to embrace and use the great master key to riches:

- Mastering your tongue by controlling yourself to think before speaking, making sure that what you have to say will benefit you and not hurt others

- Not striking back those you may have a grievance with. Remember, everything you do to or for others, you're really doing to or for yourself

- Exercise self-discipline over all your emotions, particularly emotions of **LOVE, HATE, FEAR,** and **SEX**. These are the big four emotions and **they can make or break you** according to the level of discipline you exercise over them

- Your mental attitude must be controlled all the time since it can bring physical or mental illness if uncontrolled, and may make peace of mind impossible

- Exercise self-discipline over the **emotion of sex** because it can be responsible for a person's failure. This **is the most powerful of all the emotions**. By controlling this particular emotion, one can achieve their major purpose in life

- Your stomach also needs discipline through appropriate dieting and fasting

- Exercise self-discipline in relation to religion and politics. You must be able to live and let live. You must allow others to also have the same privileges that you are demanding for yourself

- The most important of all self-discipline is: Taking possession of your own mind and directing it to what you may desire. It's so simple that its use doesn't need a genius or any kind of education. It only requires the will to take possession of one's own mind and a definite purpose to which the mind is directed

Note that self-discipline is recommended by all religions on earth. No one becomes wiser without self-discipline. You cannot find peace of mind without the strict exercise of self-discipline. Self-discipline helps us change the hate of others into sympathy for them.

Self-discipline can give us freedom from the fear of death by mastering our fears, can save us from the fear of imaginary illnesses, and can help us live free from all kinds of limitations.

The Creator never gave us assets without the means to achieve what we desire. He gave us self-discipline as a means to control our thoughts. A positive mental attitude can clear all obstacles standing between you and your major purpose in life.

You must do the following to keep your mind positive:

- Learn to relate with others by understanding and connecting with their interests

- Refuse to be distracted by trivial things and refuse to allow them to become controversial incidents in your relations with others

- Set a reminder to keep your mind alert and positive from morning till bedtime, regardless of circumstances

- Learn to sell yourself to others by indirection by asking leading questions

- Do not engage in arguments over unimportant subjects

- Adopt a habit of a good heart or laugh every time you feel angry

- Start your day by exercising a good laugh to set yourself on a positive mental attitude throughout the whole day

- Express gratitude for all the adversities and defeats you have gone through in the past

- Give thanks for the blessings you expect to receive during the day

- Focus on the "can-do" and act on them promptly. No matter the level of your problems, there is always something you can do there and then. You need to find out what action you need to take and do it promptly

- Decide on a good habit to switch your mind to whenever you experience some unpleasant moments. When you feel anger, switch your mind to your major purpose in life

- Every situation that comes your way, whether pleasant or not, is an opportunity for growth. Use it to make yourself some dividends in one form or another. Remember, your strength grows out of your struggles. Once you master this, you will soon realize that there is no such a thing as an uncomfortable experience

- Look upon your life as a continuous process of education, as an opportunity of learning from all your experiences whether good or bad

- Be always on the alert for gains of wisdom coming to you through pleasant or unpleasant experiences

- Express gratitude at least twice a day for the fact that God has given you the means for complete control over your own mind and ask for guidance to use this power wisely in all your thoughts and acts

- Go out of your way to comment positively about others; your colleagues, your family. Do not mention their negative qualities, then observe how quickly people will start to concentrate on your own good qualities

- Accept all criticism of yourself as an occasion for self-examination and an opportunity for self-discovery, which will help you through the remainder of your life

- Do not accept from life or anyone anything you do not desire. Gandhi proved himself to be more powerful than the Great British military forces through the simple method of passive resistance

- Remember that there are two kinds of circumstances which will cause you to worry. There are the ones you can do something about, and others you can't do anything about. For some, you can use passive resistance and for others, you can refuse to allow them to bother you

- Keep your mind internally engaged, thinking about what you desire most, your major purpose in life. No time will be left to think about what you do not want

- If you ever feel sorry for yourself, look around and find someone worse off than yourself and help them. Make this a habit and you will witness great miracles in life. Because that which you do for another, you do for yourself

- Choose some individual who you consider the kind of person you'd like to be. Do your best to emulate that person in every way possible. Great people have always been hero admirers. They pick the right kinds of people to emulate

- Work on your tone of voice so that it has a pleasing musical sound. Remember that the sound of your voice is a means for other people to look into your soul. Record yourself daily and find your voice. If you're engaged in selling, this practice will result in monetary dividends

- Paste this sentence on your bathroom mirror or at your office: "Whatever the mind can conceive and believe, the mind can achieve"

- Remember that you are the only person who can provide you with a positive mental attitude. What are you going to do about it?

"Your entire future rests on this question. We are now rubbing elbows with the great master key to success!"

The seventh principle: Enthusiasm

Emotions are not directly subject to reason, but to action. We can achieve nothing until we express enthusiasm.

How to develop a feeling of enthusiasm for all that you do?

Enthusiasm can be likened to steam and boiler, one of which is controlled and turned on to start the wheels of a machine into action.

Knowledge is power. This is only half true!

"Knowledge becomes true power when it is put into action for the attainment of a definite objective."

Enthusiasm is a powerful means to put into action our education, experience and knowledge. Acting without enthusiasm may be ineffective and boresome.

Why does enthusiasm affect the mind of those who come under your influence?

Your brain is a broadcasting station in communication with the receiving stations. The broadcasting station sends out vibrations that are picked up by the receiving stations. When you turn on enthusiasm, your thoughts reach out very quickly to the receivers.

"This is a fact known to psychologists for ages and is still being used by top salesmen today."

Enthusiasm is very contagious and engages all those who come under its influence. It causes them to feel the enthusiasm as well. Be careful, because enthusiasm, whether constructive or destructive, is still contagious!

Enthusiasm is a necessary trait for leadership

Some employers look for people who can express themselves with intense enthusiasm when they want to hire leaders for managerial positions.

Most successful lawyers are not necessarily those who know the most about the legal profession, but those who know how to influence courts and juries and have a great capacity of expressing themselves with enthusiasm.

When you are introduced to someone, you have an opportunity to sell yourself favorably to that person. When you shake hands, use the opportunity to make a favorable impression of yourself based on the level of enthusiasm you put in that handshake.

Top salesmen's use of enthusiasm

When you meet someone and you'd like to make a favourable impression of yourself, whether it is for the first time or someone you're already acquainted with, do these things:

- Use an enthusiastic tone of voice to make the other person realize you are happy to communicate with him or her

- When you shake hands, use a firm grip

- If you must say something, be sure to direct your conversation to their interest

- Follow through by eagerly asking questions that will keep up the attention, then when it is your turn to say something about what you are bringing to the table, the other person will be prepared to listen attentively

- The best way to sell yourself to others is to sell others to themselves

- Selling is the world's highest-paid profession and every company needs a top-notch and enthusiastic salesman

Enthusiasm is an expression of a positive mental attitude

One doctor recognized that the enthusiasm he brought with him into the room of a sick person had more healing power than all the medications he could prescribe.

Worry can bring all sorts of illnesses, and its cure is a positive mental attitude. Disease has no place in the body of a person who is always positive.

Another very important and powerful aspect of enthusiasm

Prayer expressed with intense enthusiasm brings much faster and more satisfying results. Try it for yourself and be convinced.

I would like to end this chapter by asking you to join me in the following prayer:

"Dear God, you are my All Divine Providence, I thank you for all your provision, I ask not for more riches, but for more wisdom with which to use wisely the riches you gave me at birth, to make wiser use of the power to control my own mind, my life and whatever I desire."

Be humble, sincere, and embrace a better world!

Please note: This world is fixed to prevent the weak from losing and not the strong from winning, which is why it is so much easier to make a living and support a family than it is to become rich.

With all the security and social assistance systems in place to help the weak, it's up to you to set your goals above the set threshold and pursue the life of your dreams!

Remember:

"Knowledge becomes true power when it is put into action for the attainment of a definite goal."

Ready to take action for your success in life and business?

What's The Most Appropriate And Effective Action To Take Now?

Introduction to the number one internet marketing program - Discover the most powerful all-in-one page and funnel creation software and the most effective sales and affiliate platform

Questions:

- Are you living your ideal life?

- What's your interest? Is it about:

- How to start your home-based online business with little investment?

- How to run your fitness business online

- Drop-shipping, how to start an e-commerce business and be able to sell other people's products online without dealing with storage, inventory and shipping and without breaking the bank?

- How to leverage the rising power of social media marketing to promote your products or services through Facebook, YouTube, Instagram, Twitter, Pinterest, LinkedIn, etc

- How to make regular income on the stock market

- How to efficiently manage your Real Estate business online

- How to manage your financial consultancy business online

- How to start or grow your marketing agency

- How to start your own network marketing business

- How to write a book in a few days and how to self-publish

- How to sell on Amazon, etc.

- Are you ready to decide that enough is enough?

- READY TO TAKE ACTION?

How would you like to be introduced to my mentor and his team of experts to hold your hand through customized training that comes with practical tools to help you build a successful business and turn your life around completely while doing your 30-day challenge? **(All for FREE NOW!).**

Mike Filsaime and his team of experts have created what is being labelled as the "Michael Jordan" or the "Steve Jobs" version of internet marketing programs. They have created the fastest-growing software platforms for digital and eCommerce marketers thanks to their enormous experience in the game.

Through his software innovations, Mike Filsaime has generated more than $125 million by following his passion while delivering game-changing software designed to overcome the major pains and frustrations related to problems such as poor traffic and conversions, faced by online entrepreneurs and marketers.

Mike holds the distinction of doing more One-Million-Dollar launches for more brands than any other marketer. Unlike most of his competitors, on top of his powerful marketing skills, Mike is first of all a software developer.

He was responsible for several well-known software platforms, such as Kartra, WebinarJam, PayDotCom,

Butterfly Marketing, EverWebinar, EvergreenBusiness System, and DealGuardian.

As a gesture of kindness during this COVID19 crisis, which is still affecting people today, Mike Filsaime and his partners have decided to help other fellow entrepreneurs by giving LIFETIME FREE ACCESS to the number one all-in-one platform every entrepreneur or marketer needs to build their businesses.

By taking advantage of this amazing offer today, you will also have access to free tutorials and be able to learn why GrooveFunnels is currently the best on the market. You will have the chance to learn how you can start making residual income through GrooveAffiliate without paying a dime.

You will learn about GrooveMember (for your membership sites), GrooveMail (integrated autoresponder for email marketing), GroovePages (for building your funnels or your classic websites), GrooveSell, GrooveVideo (which works like Vimeo), GrooveWebinar (now you can run your webinars on the same platform as your funnels), GrooveBlog (SEO-friendly, unlike many other platforms).

GrooveFunnels is currently scoring higher than platforms such as Clickfunnels and any others in terms of affordability, user-friendly, performance, customer service and many other aspects, therefore making it the number one funnel building software.

Considering the 40% first tier affiliate compensation plan and the 10% second tier, this is a powerful sales and affiliate program that anyone can start promoting for free today regardless of their education, business or location in the world.

You will also have a chance to be introduced to GrooveKart which is the best eCommerce, print-on-demand and drop-shipping platform on the market today. With a few clicks, you can start selling products online today with no need for warehousing, shipping or inventory.

At the moment, GrooveKart is more robust and a much more affordable platform than Shopify.

To build your business on GrooveDigital software you do not have to be a web developer or tech-savvy. All the GrooveDigital platforms are user-friendly.

If managing your business under one roof is important to you, this is the platform of your dreams (no more dependency on third party software such as Zoom, ActiveCampaign, etc…). In case you still prefer holding on to these other platforms, you will be glad to know that they can all integrate with GrooveFunnels with a simple drag and drop technique.

Whether you're an experienced marketer or you're still trying to figure out your way around this powerful and revolutionary marketing technique using customized sales funnels… or you're a newbie to entrepreneurship and not sure yet what product to sell. **Take advantage of this offer while you still can. Go ahead and open your FREE account at www.affiliateprogramsforbeginners.com. (FREE to join now!)**

No credit card is needed to get your lifetime access to this powerful platform today. **It's all free and there is no upsell, which will save you a whopping $99 per month for life!**

You will have access to free customized training to help you succeed, no matter where you live on this planet or your level of education or even your type of business.

You can start applying the lessons you're learning in this book today and launch your business online right now **without spending a single dollar.**

Most rewarding affiliate programs

As a gesture of compassion to overcome the COVID-19 crisis, here is the link to the most powerful and highly rewarding affiliate programs on the market for you to take advantage of and start making residual or passive income for yourself today; **you need to go to:** https://eprofitmethods.com. **(FREE to join now!)**

Made-for-you software or funnels for selling your products or services

Designing funnels can be time-consuming and may even be frustrating for many people. To make your life easier, my team and I have built the highest-converting software and made-for-you funnels that are ready to use. You just need to plug in your products or services, and you are good to start running your business on the best internet marketing system. **To get started today, go to www.jobsrendezvous.com.**

Info products ready-made for you with commercial rights

Many entrepreneurs lose focus while trying to figure out what to sell. I know I did when I started! Building products from scratch is one of the main drawbacks faced by entrepreneurs.

A lot of businesses fail even before takeoff, as entrepreneurs are, for the most part, overwhelmed by tasks such as fundraising, setting up and running marketing campaigns, etc. ... while they are still trying to focus on bringing their product to life.

To fulfil our mission of helping fellow entrepreneurs achieve success (the same way we were also assisted), my team and I have come up with the most sought-after products (mainly info products) ready for you to grab and resell with full rights. **Would you like to have access to the most sought after products already made for you with all the commercial rights for you to rebrand and use as your own ? To find them now, go to:** www.andymutambya.com.

Is it easy?

Depending on your determination, you may find it easy or difficult.

Is it for everyone?

Only you can tell! If you say YES, you're right, and if you say NO, you're right too! It's all up to you and how committed you are to turn your life around.

Resources recommended by the Author

Ready to tap into the growing number of online business opportunities and claim your share in the billion dollar industry? Whether you're a newbie or experienced online entrepreneur or marketer, regardless of your nationality, location, type of business or level of education, you will find all you need here:

www.affiliateprogramsforbeginners.com

https://eprofitmethods.com/

www.jobsrendezvous.com

www.andymutambya.com

For more on recurring income ideas, opportunities, and inspirational messages, I'd like to invite you to check out my Facebook and Instagram pages by searching for "Andy Mutambya". May I also ask you to like and comment?

One more challenge for you: Would you like to grow and succeed with others just like you by being accountable to each other?

If you decide to take part in this challenge, you will be entitled to join our new Facebook group made up of ambitious and hard-working world-changers. Search on Facebook for (Highest Paying Affiliate Program) to join our group. You will be able to share and learn more from other entrepreneurs on a continual basis and grow with the best.

Remember to leave a comment about how the 30-day and 7-day tests are working out for you, including other challenges, trainings and products mentioned in this book. Your comment will help inspire others. Once you're accepted in the group, please type "YES" in the comment to confirm your willingness to participate in this challenge!

If this book helps you in any way, would you like to leave a helpful review on our Amazon book page, "Think To Grow Rich – Applying The Laws Of Success And The Power Of Habit In 2020 (Overcoming COVID-19 Crisis) - by Andy Mutambya." Would you also consider leaving your supportive comment on our Facebook page?

Please note that part of the income generated by this book is intended to be invested in non-governmental organizations with a mission to help empower vulnerable women and girls facing rape and all kinds of injustices, including affected children.

Don't forget to pass on the blessings as well. Remember, if you contribute to prosperity, you must prosper in return! It's a law!

Thank you so much for reading, and I wish you all the success you can dream of...Until we meet again, I wish you health, wealth, and peace of mind!

Andy Mutambya

Acknowledgement

I'd like to express my special gratitude to the incredible teachers who inspired me along the way, and without whom this piece of work wouldn't have been achievable.

Thank you Les Brown, Earl Nightingale, Mike Filsaime, Napoleon Hill, Tony Robbins, Zig Ziglar, Lisa Nichols, Steve Larsen, Bob Proctor, Robert Kiyosaki, Russell Brunson, Julie Stoian… for your priceless teachings and inspiration.

"Not being able to decide is a decision."
"Don't die with your music in you."